Fiat lux!

The Adventures of a
Lighthouse Keeper's Daughter.

Written by Dave Strzok

Illustrated by Randall Peterson

Author's Note:

This book was written
to be read aloud to children.
It is full of examples of life style
practices in the early half
of the 20th Century.

Edna's personal stories
can be a springboard to
sharing stories and
experiences of one's own
personal heritage with
children and
grandchildren.

Edna Lane couldn't remember much about her first arrival to Bayfield with her mother. It was May, 1902, and time to meet her father for their trip to their new home at the Michigan Island Lighthouse in the Apostle Islands. Edna was happy Father had allowed her to bring some of her favorite toys because otherwise life was going to be lonely for an eight-year-old girl 20 miles out in Lake Superior. When Father's boat entered the City Dock, Edna could see his smile from a block away. He tied up the boat while Mother ran down to the mooring and they embraced while Edna caught up. When she got there, Father lifted her high over his head and told her he had a surprise for her. Then he reached down and lifted a curly haired golden Cocker Spaniel from the boat. Edna squealed for joy when he handed her the little dog. Father had told her several times that a pet on the island would be just lonely - unless she became a good companion for him. She knew this was going to be a wonderful summer and squeezed the little dog tightly to her chest.

"What's his name, Father?" she asked.

"Well, Edna," he answered, "I think he's going to want to have a name his best friend gives him. Give it some thought, Edna. Watch what he does, how he tickles your fancy, and tell him what you'd like to call him. Then see if he comes when you call him by that name."

2

That sounded like a good idea, Edna thought, and she began to watch him closely to see what he liked to do most. First, he sniffed everything. And wiggled his tail. "Sniffy," she thought. Or "Wiggles." No, they were going to be friends for a long time and that was a puppy's name. She would think more about it.

Once the luggage was loaded into the skiff, Father turned the boat northeast, raised the main sail and the jib, and the family of three began a summer of adventure.

"Watch closely, Edna," Father said as he rigged the skiff. "This is going to be completely new for you. By the end of the summer, though, you might be able to sail alone."

"What's going to be difficult," Mother said, "is the name for all the parts of the boat. Also the wind keeps shifting so you don't know what to do next."

"The wind and all the parts of the boat are what you have to pay attention to make

3

sailboats do what you want them to do," Father answered. "You'll get the knack of it. Look at that little piece of red yarn on the mainstay, that line running up to the top of the mast. That flows with the wind and you set your sails to catch the wind on the side. Or, to stop, you can turn into the wind and the sails will luff because you pinched the angle too much, then to gain way, you have to fall off a little bit and fill up the sails again or the boat will stop."

"When I was in the navy," Father explained, "they told us that sailors named every object on a boat in two ways: one for the location of the object, one for the function of the object. So the 'bow' is the front of the boat. The 'stern' is the back. The left side is called 'port,' and the right side is called 'starboard.' These are old mariners' words. On the right, since most men were right-handed, they placed the 'steer board' or the tiller. Eventually it became 'starboard,' because sailors came from all coastal nations

 4

and spoke different languages and pronounced words differently. In order to keep from banging and breaking the steerboard against the docks, they would land the left side of the boat on the dock, and that was the port side. And the 'port' is where you tie your boat up."

Edna liked the new words and new ideas which they taught her. "Pinch" was funny. "Falling off" wasn't, she decided.

"Why do they call it 'falling off,'?" Edna asked.

"Because the bow of the boat 'falls off' from the direction of the wind," Father replied.

Well, it all made sense without even knowing what the words meant, Edna thought. This was going to be fun.

"Where does the wind come from, Father?" Edna asked.

"In the navy, they taught us how weather flows into the area where warm air is rising. That's usually on the land," Father explained .

5

"Then that movement of air is what we call wind."

That made sense. Now, what made it fast or slow, she wondered, but in the meantime, she watched her new buddy and watched the sails, and that was enough for what Father called a "landlubber." He'd learned that in the navy, too. They must have pronounced their words differently. Father explained that it really meant "landlover," those people who liked to be on land.

The trip to the island was gentle and very slow, about 5 miles an hour, Father said. Edna did the mathematics in her head: "Five miles an hour times 20 miles equals four hours." Her mother, standing beside Father at the tiller, showed a pleased smile when Edna announced the duration of the sail. They would be there by early afternoon, plenty of time to settle into their new quarters.

The islands were spring gray, except for the tall pines, but she could imagine how they would look when the leaves finally dressed out the trees. Oak Island was very tall, Stockton Island stretched out to the northeast, while Madeline Island, the largest, extended along almost sixteen miles of their trip.

Finally, they arrived at the beach below the white tower of the new lighthouse. No one was there to meet them and they crawled up all 103 steps, four times, before they had carried all their travel trunks to the top. Then Mother immediately looked around, locating a garden site for vegetables and one for flowers she would plant over the next month, just in time for summer growth and fresh food.

Edna, ever mindful of the new companion Father had given her, noticed the unmistakable characteristic she was waiting for: her little dog ran, all the time, sniffing every bush and shrub, wagging his stubby tail until it seemed like the tail was wagging him rather than the other way around. He was Runny. No question what he did most, and almost constantly.

The first night on the island was wonderful, beginning with the long, slow sunset as the red ball sank into the hills back near Bayfield. Mother made up a blanket mattress in the corner of the kitchen, small enough so that it could be rolled up and stowed behind the wood box during the day. The kitchen was very tidy, with open shelves for dishes and cooking supplies. The wood box was full of dry, split maple and kindling to start the cooking fire, and there was a hand pump in the east window from which Mother drew fresh water. One door led to Mother and Father's room. One door led to the light tower.

Edna fell asleep easily, hoping Runny would be happy in his spot beneath the steps which led into the north door of the lighthouse. She would check him in the morning to see whether

he needed anything, like pine needles for soft
bedding. Father pointed out that she could find
some "duff," or pine needles, beneath the big
white pines north of the house. Father also
pointed out that two eagles would come and sit
in the tallest of the pines almost every day.

Edna wondered whether Mother would let her sleep with Runny some night, when it warmed up later in the summer. She was sure her dog was going to learn to love her. By morning, the spring winds had shifted to the northeast and it was chilly and damp. She stayed cuddled under the covers until Mother called her to breakfast. She hadn't heard Father get up to tend the light six times, as was his required duty. Perhaps by the end of the summer, she could get up with him to see the night stars and he would tell her how he learned the stars' names while he was in the navy before she was born. She already knew Polaris, the north star, which mariners used to tell their direction on clear nights.

When Edna asked Father why the wind got so cold, he explained that the wind shifted to the north and got cooled by the cold lake water. Then he told her some of the rhymes sailors used to forecast weather.

"Red skies at night, sailors' delight. Red sky

in the morning, sailors take warning."

"Why does that work, Father?" Edna asked.

"Because there are tiny moisture particles in the air, and they make the sunlight red when the sun drops low to the horizon. If you look up in the sky, Edna," he went on, "you can see the low clouds hurrying towards the southwest. In about two hours, the fast wind that pushes those clouds will drop to the level of the lake and the waves on the lake will start to build, the air will cool, the temperature will drop, and there will probably be a fog because clouds are made out of the tiny moisture particles.

Edna sure was learning a lot about the earth when Father explained it that way. He always knew she would ask, "why?" and he sometimes answered her question before she could ask it.

Mother made oatmeal for breakfast, an easy warm start to what would become the first of many busy lightkeeper days. In a few days, a boat from Bayfield would bring out a tan and white milk cow and calf and they would share fresh milk with the calf. In the meantime, they would drink their milk out of a can which Father called the Tin Cow. Fresh milk would taste far better. They would be able to make butter to put into the cool root cellar beneath the kitchen floor, and Mother would put it on freshly baked bread for almost every meal.

Edna spent the day following Runny around the island's trails that loggers had cut in previous years. She even discovered a stack of hemlock bark which people soaked in water in vats and then used the acid water to tan deer and cow hides. Even though Mother had cautioned her to stay on the trail and to use the sun as a direction finder, the hemlock bark wasn't very far off the trail, so Edna wasn't being unsafe. When the sun was highest overhead, Mother said Edna should be back at the lighthouse for lunch. She followed Runny, up and down banks, along the south shore of the island, along clay cliffs, over boulders and sand dunes. She thought the seagulls liked it when Runny crashed into their flock, scattering them in all directions. Then the seagulls would take their turns and chase Runny, pretending they were going to peck him on his stubby tail. By the end of summer, the gulls would see Runny start down the beach and would fly from their gathering to meet their little playmate, starting their game before Runny could get to their spot. With all that running, Edna was starving for lunch before the sun got to its highest place in the sky. Runny must have been hungry, too, because his trot back to the lighthouse was more direct with fewer stops at the bushes and shrubs.

Lunch was a sandwich of jam and butter that Mother had warmed on the stove when she saw the little girl and her dog come into the lighthouse clearing.

13

Over lunch, Father told how the lighthouse had been built in 1854, and how the inspector refused to accept the building, insisting that the builder had put it on the wrong island. Edna couldn't imagine how you could build a lighthouse on the wrong island, but the builder was made to build another one on Long Island like he was supposed to in the first place. Father told about how he had known of several buildings being built in the wrong places when he was in the navy. A lighthouse in the wrong place could be dangerous for ships traveling in the night when the crew was relying on the light to mark their course. They wouldn't be able to tell where they were. Each lighthouse, he explained, had a specific flash and dark time, a span of time created by the turning lantern table, which turned, according to Father, because of weights on long chains which dropped slowly by gravity and spun the lens.

When the Lighthouse inspector rejected the

light, he turned it off and abandoned it for nine years, then relit the light, deciding, after all, that Michigan Island was a good light for leading ships among the islands to Chequamegon Bay. To help us remember the name of the bay, Father told the story about a Chippewa chief who walked down to the lake in mid summer, stuck his big toe in the water and said: "She warm again," and that made the strange name easy to recall. Chippewa, Father explained, were one of the three main Indian tribes which lived in this area when the White settlers arrived.

"What does Chequamegon mean?" Edna asked her father.

"It's a Chippewa word for 'soft beaver dam,'" Father explained. "Their legend says that Winibijou, the original man, wanted to trap a beaver in the bay, so he built a soft beaver dam around the narrow part, hoping to make the beaver come out of the water. But the wind and waves conspired against him and washed an

15

opening for the beaver to swim out underwater, and he escaped. In frustration, Winibijou threw clods of dirt after the fleeing beaver and they fell into the lake and made the Apostle Islands."

Edna liked that story and would write it in her diary. She liked to draw pictures of each story to help her imagine what was going on.

Within the first week of their arrival on Michigan Island, Mother and Edna began staking out the flower and vegetable gardens, a round one just west of the house and a much larger rectangular one mostly for vegetables, each variety becoming ready to eat and can throughout the summer. Around the round garden, Father put small white stones arranged to make N, E, S, W, around the edge, so that they would know the map directions from their lighthouse. That way they could easily tell which direction the wind blew from.

Mother put onions and carrots in first, showing Edna how to press each plant into

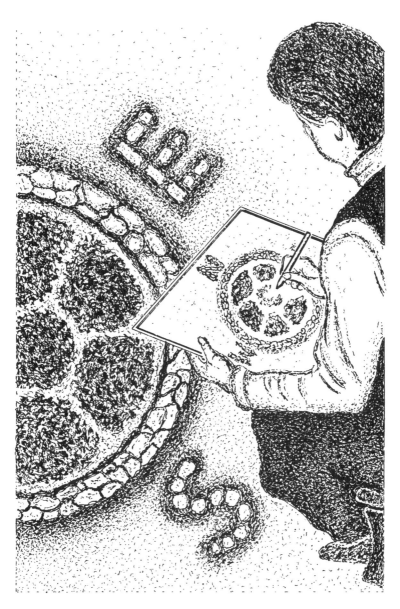

the softened soil, three inches apart, all in a straight row. The next row was carrots, whose tiny seeds had to be sprinkled individually into the v-shaped cavities laid out by Mother's goose-neck hoe. Then Edna gently covered the seeds with an inch of soil and tapped the soil down to cover each one safely from the gulls which like to search in newly tilled soils looking for seeds and grubs. Radishes came next, planted much like the carrots, then leaf lettuce, then peas, green beans, squash, corn and cabbage. Onions would be ready to eat first, and when they were picked, three would be taken out and one left to grow to its full size. Mother wasn't sure tomatoes would reach maturity because of the short growing season, but she felt the lake might protect them longer from freezing in the fall and wanted to try them. Finally, Mother showed Edna the hills she mounded up for potatoes, dug a hole in the center of each mound and had Edna drop one

18

cut piece of seed potato, each with one eye pointing up, then they covered each, patted the hill firmly and began to sprinkle the garden each evening with rainwater from the barrel under the eaves of the house.

Every day Edna would examine the growth of the plants, noticing how much they grew from day to day. By the end of June, they were harvesting radishes, onions, leaf lettuce and small carrots. The potatoes needed to be watched for potato bugs so that they wouldn't eat the leaves and deprive the potatoes of nutrients from the sun. Through all this, Runny would lie in the shade of trees, remembering how Edna had scolded him the first time he walked into the garden. Edna even lifted his ear to remind him several more times: "Keep Out!" He still went back at night and sniffed around the plants to see what she made such a big fuss over. The onions looked like they were the only plants which had a chance, but they sure stunk .

By June, Edna and Runny would head down the trails, searching for strawberry and then raspberry plants to ripen. Mother would send along a basket for Edna to collect the berries in. For the first few days, berries were scarce and Mother told Edna to eat what she wished, just like Chippewa children would do when they went foraging for food. They didn't sit down to meals like city people did. They just ate as they walked the trails. Once the berries were fully ripened, there was no way Edna could eat all the berries and she began to take them home for jams, sauces, juice and for ingredients in pancakes and muffins. The garden seemed to have new plants to harvest every day, and with the fresh trout and whitefish Father netted offshore, their meals were wonderful.

The laying hens which fishermen had brought out with the cow and calf hatched their chicks and Runny had to be taught not to chase them, mainly because he'd get his nose pecked.

20

Mother offered to let Edna milk the cow once but she couldn't co-ordinate her squeeze to get the milk to come out. She learned how to give milk mixed with water to the calf, how to strain the dirt out of the milk, how to ladle the cream off the top of the milk after it had cooled and how to stir it to make butter. Mother promised she would show her how to make cottage cheese once the calf started eating grass and took less milk. That would be later in the summer.

Mother's flower garden blossomed all summer and into the fall. She tended that mostly alone but would call Edna to look at new blossoms when a flower finally joined the rest of the display. Mother explained that she would silently thank each flower for its beauty after it had passed its peak, because she knew this was simply part of passing on what each part of creation gave best to a beautiful world. One of Mother's favorite writers was Henry David Thoreau, who wrote a piece explaining how life and death as God created it was perfect. She recited it to Edna many times, and she knew she should remember it because it was so important to Mother: "Every leaf in the forest, every blade in the field gives up its life as perfectly as it takes it up."

While pointing out the new blossoms, Mother pointed out how bees would visit different flowers every day and she wanted Father to follow the trail of bees to the honey tree while they were still busy. Then they would take some for home use. Edna wasn't interested in digging into the hive because she knew from the mosquitoes and gnats that getting stung was going to hurt, then itch for a long time after that. Father, on the other hand, said he would do it and put on a long-sleeved shirt, a hat tied around his face with his pant legs stuffed into his boots and rob the hive the morning of the first frost in the fall, when the bees were beginning to be dormant later and later into the day.

As Father led Edna to the bee tree, a hollow old trunk behind the lighthouse, he taught her that each bee had a particular job to do in the hive: worker bees collected nectar from blossoms, drones took care of the queen bee, and she laid all the eggs in the cones. There could only be one queen bee in a hive, he pointed out, and two or more queens would fight with each other until only one survived. Edna watched bees gather nectar several times, and she noticed how the worker bees would get fuzzy yellow furs when they crawled in and out of the blossoms. Mother pointed out that if the bees didn't do that on every blossom, the plants, including apple and plum trees, would never bear fruit.

"The wind helps carry pollen," Father told her, "but when bees enter the flower, they carry pollen from the last plant they were in to the new plant, and that starts the process of making the small fruits."

Edna couldn't imagine why this was necessary, but she accepted what Father said and would watch to see how that happened.

That fall, Edna watched Father's bravery from the distance, but it worked just like he said. The buckets of honey were really messy looking, but Edna dipped into the honey every chance she had. Mother showed her how to melt the wax of the honeycombs and they began to make candles which they used during the fall evenings before going to bed.

Edna's days with Runny were as full of as much variety as Edna could imagine. Sometimes they would simply stroll in a berry patch going from bush to bush. Runny would try a berry sometimes, at Edna's urging, but he generally snorted and flopped his ears in distaste. Fair enough, Edna thought, she didn't eat angle worms that came slithering out at

24

night and Runny did. She picked the worms up
and put them into Mother's compost pile where
she threw the vegetable pieces and the worms
would eat the stalks and help make rich soil for
the gardens next year. Edna learned that angle
worms would crawl out on the surface of the
ground when it rained a lot, because otherwise
they could drown. She learned that watching
the robins in the springtime. They knew how to
pick an easy meal. Edna made a drawing of a
robin eying the worm out of one eye, then he
yanked the worm out and delivered it to the

25

young robins in the cedar tree. When the robin turned its head to eye a worm, Edna thought the robin might be listening to the tiny 'pop' of the worm as the bubble popped as the worm left its hole. "Robins are some of the first local birds to come to nest in the spring," Father told Edna. "We start thinking about planting gardens when they get here. Their food is largely earthworms, so the ground has to be thawed for them to get enough food to feed their young, so if the ground is thawed, we can start planting gardens. All sorts of animals tell us about seasonal changes. Tiny spring peepers, squeaky little frogs in spring, tell us the frost is out of the ground because reptiles need the warmth of the sun to get energy until the bugs and flies come out to give the reptiles energy when they eat them."

"Gosh, Father, nature seems to have it all worked out. Are there any other special birds around here?" Edna asked her father.

"Yes," he answered, "We have the eagles. But eagles come in pairs during February and either return to last year's nests or build a new one in a safe area. We have a pair of eagles on Michigan Island. What's very special is that the eagle is our nation's bird."

Edna asked Father why sometimes in artwork you would see an eagle with arrows and a bunch of grain in its claws.

"That's a symbol of our nation," he answered. "The arrows stand for war and protecting our land from invaders, and the grain is to show we grow grain for some of our food. And you will also notice on a coin, that 'In God we trust' is written there. That's to remind us that God's creation will take care of us if we do our fair share of the work." Edna studied the coin Father used to show her the symbols, and she knew the eye in a triangle was God.

Fly season kept Edna and Mother in the house except for the early morning and late evening cool, when the sand flies went off duty and the mosquitoes came out. Runny was generally miserable then with flies biting him when he least expected it. Mother noticed bloody spots on his tender nose and she had Edna smear bag balm on it which she put on the cow's udder. Runny reacted the same way as he did with berries, only he snorted louder. Mother did the same thing for the cow and calf because those black flies could sure make themselves irritating. Edna would always watch to see that the cow wouldn't lick it off her nose with her big long tongue and she usually stopped licking after she tasted the smelly grease.

The garden grew wonderfully and Edna enjoyed tearing out the weeds by their roots, shaking out the garden soil and flinging the plant into the woods. She knew her help was important and Mother promised her a garden of her own next summer if she planned it out wisely. Just as Mother had hoped, the tomatoes and squash came out full of fruit, with both being stored in the cool crawl space for weeks after they were picked. Potatoes and carrots were placed in a sand pit Father had created and they could be used long after snowfall if they were not dug out of the sand. They could even be used as seed plants for the next spring.

When the lighthouse inspector's boat, the AMARANTH arrived, they sounded the ship's horn and the inspector rowed ashore. The Michigan Island lighthouse keeper's family was in the middle of the noon meal and there wasn't enough time to clean the house and wash the dishes, so Mother stuffed the dishes in the oven and hoped he wouldn't look there. Mostly he just delivered new library books to Mother, led Father around, and walked up the tower to the light. Edna and Runny walked in among the apple trees and watched for Mother to call them. At the end of his short visit, the inspector called Edna over and examined her fingernails and asked to see her teeth. He knew that if her parents were not wise enough to take good care of their daughter's health, they certainly wouldn't be taking good care of the lighthouse.

During blueberry season, around the Fourth of July, berries would be plentiful on Stockton Island. The fishermen called it 'Presqu'ile'" because the peninsula they lived on was "almost an island." The Chippewa name for the island was "Burnt Wood Island," because they burned blueberry bushes in early spring and the new growth produced more berries. The Chippewa canoes were already coming from Madeline Island with women and children to pick the berries. Mother and Edna were taken to the island early one day with baskets for the berries, stayed all day and were picked up in the early evening. The summer days were at their longest then because they had just passed the summer solstice, the time of year when North America was closest to the sun.

Edna's first visit to another lighthouse was

30

on the Fourth of July when all the lighthouse keepers got together on Raspberry Island. Raspberry Island had been picked because it was so homey, the flower gardens were in full bloom and wives thought it was most beautiful and like a home on the mainland. Mother was gracious enough to allow that Raspberry's gardens were magnificent but she agreed with Father that Michigan Island's garden was as beautiful as any garden they had seen.

All the lightkeepers of the Apostle Islands brought their families except for the Outer and Devils Island men who were bachelors. There were five keeper's children and they immediately began to compare stories. Roberta, from Sand Island lighthouse, was about Edna's age, so they became friends right away.

"How long have you been coming out to the islands?" Edna asked.

"Only three years," Roberta replied. "and next year we'll be back again. My father thinks if he does a good job by himself, we can stay on Sand Island most of our lives."

"Do you have any pets, Edna?" Roberta asked.

"Yes," she exclaimed. "I have a cocker spaniel named 'Runny.' We've become the best of friends."

Once the other children came over, their stories turned into hide and seek, then to croquet on the lawn, then it was time to eat. The keepers began gathering at the picnic table and the women carried the food baskets out and displayed their special plates: bread pudding, rice and chicken, garden salads, freshly baked bread, boiled eggs, carrots, and other vegetables. The bachelors' baskets were funny: some had linen covers which had never been unfolded before, their keeper's clothes were extra crisp and they acted very dignified among the mothers. They didn't seem to know how to act around the children and the children didn't want to go near them. Once the children got their food, they wandered off to a blanket on the grass where they could chatter among themselves and not disturb the adults. What they talked about was usually hard for the children to understand anyhow.

Once the dinner was over, the men headed toward the beach. The mothers gathered up the plates and baskets, stuffed leftovers into the bachelors' baskets, making sure they got cookies. Mother and Edna had made cookies especially for them before they came because Mother knew the men wouldn't usually bake cookies. Edna loved making cookies, watching the little dough gobs flatten out on the cookie sheets. She always wanted to make more than Mother made up. Usually Mother would let her take some of the dough and she would make shapes on her cookie sheets: a shape of Runny, seagulls and spruce trees.

After packing up the baskets, the children

led the mothers down to the shore to watch the bonfire. Father explained that in the earliest times of lighthouses, the Greeks would build fires on cliffs to guide ships to port on the Island of Pharos, and that was the first means of signaling. Lighthouse keepers were all descendants of those ancient guardians who proudly protected the coastal mariners. Father was very proud of his service aboard a navy ship and the people around him never tired of listening to his stories. He told the other keepers that when he was in the navy, he had stood watch on the USS CONSTITUTION once and had served time on the USS CHICAGO, the first all-iron US Navy ship.

By mid afternoon, the fire was nothing more than bed of glowing coals and it was time for the keepers to start back to their islands. The Outer Island bachelors and the Michigan Island boat had the farthest to travel, so they cast off and headed broadside of the wind

34

toward Michigan Island. The islands were fully dressed in green now. Oak Island stood about 400 feet above the lake. By the time the little boat rounded Oak Island's southwest sand point, Mother pointed out where Benjamin Armstrong, the famous Chippewa agent, lived. They looked for signs of people at his homestead but the family was probably at a Fourth of July celebration among the Chippewa at Red Cliff. They lost their good sailing wind behind Oak Island and Father took that opportunity to tell about the pirates in this area. They called themselves the Twelve Apostles and would prey on the boats passing through the West Channel which found themselves becalmed when the wind died behind Oak Island. The hills on both sides of this channel were so tall that the winds would skip right over this channel, making the men in small boats turn out their oars.

Edna loved Father's stories about this area and listening to him was more interesting than reading books. She had tried to understand Longfellow's book THE SONG OF HIAWATHA, but he was writing about so many things that were old history about this area that she couldn't keep the characters and places straight in her mind. Mother helped Edna understand the part which applied to our area and Edna was determined to learn that part of the poem: "On the shores of gitchie gumee, by the shining Big-Sea-Water, stood Nokomis looking westward, ever westward." Nokomis was standing at Sault Sainte Marie on the east end of Lake Superior and he was urged by a megis shell to lead his band of Chippewa to Madeline Island, "The Home of the Yellow-Breasted Woodpecker." The Lighthouse Service library included the poems written by Henry Wadsworth Longfellow. From all of what Longfellow wrote and from what Edna's mother

36

had read, Edna liked the opening of his poem "Evangeline" the best: "This is the forest primeval." That line reminded her of the forest north of the Michigan Island lighthouse where the loggers had left a virgin forest Father called the lighthouse reserve. Edna loved that phrase, "forest primeval," and the other phrase from Longfellow's poem which Mother often read to her at bedtime was from "The Children's Hour:" "Between the dark and the daylight." She wrote these phrases in her diary because the word images were so beautiful. These wouldn't get any better if they were accompanied by drawings.

When they sailed past Hermit Wilson's Island, Father pointed out where the grouchy old man had lived and told how Wilson had gotten expelled from Madeline Island after he fought with Judge Bell and lost. Wilson continued to make herring barrels for the fishermen but the fishermen told Father he once chased some people off his island at gun point who were just wanting to sightsee. People stopped going there until John Prentice built a cabin there for his fussy high society New York bride. Mother commented about her being 19 years old. Mr. Prentice was 70, and she didn't see how that marriage was ever going to be happy. "Two people who get married should have similar interests and similar backgrounds," Mother said, "or it's not likely they will ever become friends."

Edna knew Mother and Father were friends because they always helped each other when their days' tasks tired them out and they were happy to get help and encouragement from each other with their chores. Edna felt happy for them and knew their hugs expressed happiness for everyone in the little family.

When the little boat approached Michigan Island, Runny came bounding along the shore to meet them. Edna could hear his

high-pitched bark almost before she could see
him. Once they climbed to the top of the cliff
to their home, Father said it was time to clean
the lens, trim the wick and light the light. Father
asked Edna to help him for the first time that
summer and she made note of every detail in
the process. First they wiped the crystal lens
gently with a cotton cloth, then Father trimmed
the wick, picked up a shiny brass lamp, called a
lucerne, lit the wick with a match and pushed
the burning wick into the wick at the center of
the lens. "There. FIAT LUX!" said Father. "This
lamplighter is what some people call an Alladin's
lamp," he continued. "'Wickies,' or lighthouse
keepers, call it a lucerne. One of the nicknames
for lighthouse keepers is 'Wickie,' Father pointed out, "because we always keep an eye on the
wick to make sure it doesn't make black smoke
and dirty the lens. If that happens, the light
can't be seen by the ship crews and the ship can
lose its way."

"What does 'fiat lux' mean, Father?" Edna asked.

"'Fiat lux' is God's first command in His creation of the earth. "It means 'let there be light,' in Latin," Father replied.

"Oh." She paused. "That's a lot to think about, Father." Edna finally said. She spent a few moments thinking about what "light" meant in the world. Not only was Father's job lighting the lighthouse important, but light allowed everything to live, from giving growth energy to plants to providing warmth in food for animals.

Father watched Edna solemnly look off toward the west and the slowly dying sun. Edna's eyes finally lit up again and she asked. "How do you know when to light the lamp, Father?"

"That's a good question, Edna, "Father replied. "Come stand here out on the outside of the tower."

 40

They both bent down and crawled through the small doorway onto the walkway. Edna looked down at the gardens below and backed up to the tower, away from the edge.

"That's a good thing to be cautious about, Edna," Father noted. "Just don't lean over the edge. Now hold your hand up at arms length, with your fingers out straight. Turn your hand so you can see your palm, and count the fingers between the bottom of the sun and the horizon. How many fingers?"

"Two," replied Edna.

"Good," Father continued. "We estimate

fifteen minutes for every finger between the sun and the horizon. We wait until thirty minutes before the sun goes down, then we light and trim the lamps. Now you're ready to be a lighthouse keeper, Edna."

Edna was very proud that her father would teach her how to do these important things. They bent down again and crawled into the tower.

"What kind of oil do you burn in the lamp, Father?" Edna asked.

"Asking questions is one of the most important things you'll every learn to do, Edna. This is whale oil," Father explained. "It's a very fine oil whalers get from boiling the blubber of whales. Then they put it in special cans and boats deliver it to all the lighthouses in North America. Most of it comes from Nantucket in Massachusetts. That's one of the main whaling ports in our country."

Edna liked that word "blubber." It explained exactly what the stuff probably looked like. She liked sailors' language.

Edna's father adjusted the flame until its light glowed against the inside frame of the tower. He then began cranking up the weights, released the brake and the lens began to rotate. Michigan Island lighthouse was "On Duty" for another beautiful night.

After Edna got into her nightshirt, she found her bed rolled out beside the steps next to Runny's bed. Mother finally thought she was ready to sleep out with her buddy. When she crawled under the covers, Runny wagged his tail and cuddled in beside her pillow. Nose to nose, the two little lightkeepers dozed off.

Randall Peterson is a nationally
known pointillist, having a
passionate interest in
lighthouses. He recently
presented lessons in his artistic
skills on National Public
Television in New York.
His lighthouse art is available
at the Keeper Of The Light
Nautical and Lighthouse Gift
Store in Bayfield, Wisconsin.